What Are the Winter Olympics?

by Gail Herman

illustrated by Jake Murray

Penguin Workshop

For Sara, full of grace on and off the ice—GH

For Matt and Amanda, the sportiest
and most worldly people I know—JM

PENGUIN WORKSHOP
An imprint of Penguin Random House LLC, New York

First published in the United States of America by Penguin Workshop,
an imprint of Penguin Random House LLC, New York, 2021

Visit us online at penguinrandomhouse.com.

Library of Congress Control Number: 2021020893

Printed in the United States of America

ISBN 9780593093764 (paperback)   10 9 8 7 6 5 4 3 2 1 WOR
ISBN 9780593093771 (library binding)   10 9 8 7 6 5 4 3 2 1 WOR

Contents

What Are the Winter Olympics?

It was the 2018 Winter Olympics, held in PyeongChang, South Korea. At Phoenix Snow Park, the American snowboarder Shaun White waited for his run.

No one thought he'd win.

White grew up by the beach in San Diego. He'd always loved skateboarding and decided he could use those skills for snowboarding—and snowboard tricks. He started practicing on family trips to the San Bernardino Mountains, "dropping" into icy half-pipes built into the slopes. On these U-shaped courses, athletes ride from side to side, flipping and twisting every time they fly into the air to turn around.

Amazingly, White had previously won two gold medals, one in 2006 and the other in 2010.

But the legendary snowboarder didn't three-peat in 2014. In fact, he hadn't medaled at all. Every day since, he'd lived with the disappointment.

Now thirty-one years old, he stood at the top of the Olympic half-pipe once again.

Snowboarders in a Winter Olympics contest do many runs. White was in second place, down to his final ride. To win, he'd need to perform a trick he'd never mastered in practice.

It was the very trick, in fact, that had sent him to the hospital a year earlier for sixty-two stitches.

"Shaun White," the announcer proclaimed. "The biggest run of his life."

White adjusted his goggles and took off. He rode down the twenty-two-foot wall, then up the opposite one . . . up, up, and off the edge. He spun in the air four complete times. Then he landed back on the wall, only to do the same trick on the other side.

Making his way down the pipe, White soared off the wall again—maybe twenty feet high— turning to land smoothly. He followed this trick with his famous double McTwist 1260. White flipped head over heels—two times!—during three and a half spins. It was the same move that had won him a gold medal eight years earlier.

"Perfect!" the announcer cried excitedly.

White's final score came in at 97.75 out of 100, the highest of the day. He fell to his knees, crying.

Shaun White had won his third gold medal.

It was a milestone victory for the United States, too, its one hundredth gold medal in the history of the Winter Games. So much had changed since those first Games, when snowboarding was not even a sport.

CHAPTER 1
The 1920s: Let the Winter Games Begin

Inspired by the Summer Olympics, the Winter Olympics began in 1924. Both sprang from the same ideals—to bring together the world's best athletes and encourage peace around the globe.

The site of the first-ever winter competition was a resort town called Chamonix, in the French Alps. The outdoor opening ceremony began with a parade. There were 258 athletes, from sixteen countries. Only eleven were women. They were all figure skaters, as that was the only sport open to them. The athletes wore the cold-weather uniforms they'd compete in. Some carried skates, hockey sticks, or skis. They were raring to go.

First Winter Olympics opening ceremony, Chamonix, France, 1924

The first contest of the competition was a speed-skating race, the 500-meter. (That is about one-third of a mile around the rink.) American

Charles Jewtraw from upstate New York hadn't been interested in the Olympics at first. They didn't seem like a big deal. In fact, he'd barely trained. Jewtraw thought he couldn't possibly win. But he did, becoming the very first athlete to earn a Winter gold medal.

Charles Jewtraw

Four years later, in 1928, Switzerland hosted the second Olympics. The site, St. Moritz, was another skiing resort town.

Like so many Winter Games to come, weather played a major role.

The 1928 Winter Olympics in St. Moritz, Switzerland

The 10,000-meter race—a speed-skating event—was a little over six miles around the oval. The Norwegian skaters were favorites to win. The rules in long track skating are the same today: Many racers compete in the event, two athletes skating at a time. In the end, whoever has the fastest time of all wins gold.

An American named Irving Jaffee was pitted against the top Norwegian, Bernt Evensen, in the first round. Evensen led for the first half of the contest. But near the finish line, Jaffee caught fire. He pulled even. The top of his skate crossed the line one inch ahead of Evensen.

Surely he'd have the fastest time of all the athletes.

The track was already watery from a morning rain. Now the temperature was going up. Puddles formed. Skating grew difficult. And the official canceled the race. Americans protested. They wanted the event postponed. At least that would allow Jaffee a chance at gold. The organizers couldn't make up their minds. The Norwegians decided to go home, but not before they congratulated Jaffee. There'd been no race and no medals. But they felt he truly had earned gold.

Afterward, Jaffee's new friend Billy Fiske took him out on the town. The two had little in common. Irving Jaffee grew up in the Bronx.

Irving Jaffee and Billy Fiske

The son of poor Jewish immigrants, he'd barely left New York until now. Fiske came from a wealthy family. He spent winters at expensive ski resorts like St. Moritz, the very place he took up bobsled.

Back then, bobsleds were just flat sleds with a steering wheel. Fiske was the pilot—the driver—for a five-man team. Sixteen-year-old Fiske was the only one with sledding experience. All eyes were on the other American team. But Fiske lived for speed. And he knew the mile-long twisty ice track inside and out. There would be two runs. Whichever team had the fastest combined time would win. Fiske's team had the best time for the first run, nine-tenths of a second faster than any other sled.

The second run took place on the last day of the Games. Fiske and his team went first. Sled after sled followed. No other team matched their combined time: 3 minutes, 20.5 seconds.

Billy Fiske and his bobsled team, 1928 Winter Olympics

There was only one sled left now, US #1. If they went fast enough, they could pull out a win. The sled flew like a bullet around the curves. US #1 did have the quickest time. But it wasn't fast enough to win. Fiske and his team took gold.

There was no time for a celebration. The closing ceremony was about to begin. An official found Fiske in the crowd and handed him his gold. That was all, and that was fine with Fiske. He wasn't there for a medal. He was there for speed. Jaffee and Fiske met again at the next Olympics, in 1932. The site: Lake Placid, New York, a tiny upstate town.

Would the friends repeat their victories?

CHAPTER 2
The 1930s: Troubled Times

The year 1932 was one of the worst of the Great Depression. Many people were out of work, hungry, and poor. Some countries didn't have money to send athletes to the Games.

Homeless men during the Great Depression, 1932

Billy Fiske did lead the winning bobsled team again. But he turned down a chance to compete in the next Olympics.

Little by little, Nazi dictator Adolf Hitler had made life in Germany miserable for Jews.

Adolf Hitler

His ultimate plan was to murder them, as well as all other Jews in Europe. By the end of World War II, the Nazis succeeded in killing six million Jewish people. Speed skater Jack Shea, a two-time gold medalist, wasn't Jewish. But he refused to compete at the 1936 Games. "I knew what was going on in Germany and I didn't like it," he said later. Irving Jaffee, who had turned professional and wasn't eligible for the Olympics, wanted the United States to pull out of the Games of 1936 as a protest against Hitler. The United States decided to send a team anyway.

The Games were held in the Bavarian Alps. Hitler allowed only one Jewish athlete from Germany to compete: Rudi Ball, the star hockey player.

Rudi Ball

Billy Fiske, After the Games

Why didn't Billy Fiske compete in the '36 Games? Perhaps it's because they were held in Germany when Nazi dictator Adolf Hitler was in power. After World War II broke out in Europe, Fiske joined the British Royal Air Force. A fighter pilot—looking for speed till the end—he died when his plane was shot down.

But the biggest star at the Games was Sonja Henie.

Henie was a figure skater from Norway. These Games were her fourth Olympics. She was only eleven years old at the first Winter Games, where she came in last in her competition. Henie came from a wealthy family. She had talent, charm, and determination. She traveled around Europe, training with famous coaches.

In 1928 and '32, she won gold. Henie became the first superstar athlete of the Winter Olympics. Police had to be called when she made appearances, to keep the crowds in order. Henie's routines were graceful *and* tough. She added jumps that only men had done before. She boasted, "Most always I win," and she did. Henie won her third gold medal in '36, a women's singles figure-skating record to this day.

Sonja Henie at the 1936 Games

Henie and Hitler

Sonja Henie's Olympic legacy wasn't all gold and glory. At the Games, she seemed to support Adolf Hitler, crying "Heil [hail] Hitler" and meeting him for lunch. Norwegians were horrified. The crowd's reaction didn't bother Henie. She retired from amateur figure skating later that year and went on to Hollywood, becoming a major movie star.

Three weeks after the 1936 Winter Olympics ended, German troops marched into a region called the Rhineland. It was the first step toward World War II.

The Olympics wouldn't be held again for twelve years.

CHAPTER 3
1948–1952: After the War

The war ended in 1945, and in early 1948, the Games were held again in St. Moritz. And once again, a figure-skating star was born—this time, American Richard "Dick" Button. When Button was growing up in New Jersey, his mom wanted him to be a pianist. Button discovered he liked hockey better, and figure skating even more. He began to master bigger moves, higher jumps, faster spins.

Eventually, he competed on the biggest stage in the world.

Two days before his final routine, Button completed a new jump during practice: a double axel. The move begins in a forward skate. Then comes the jump with two and half rotations—

spins in the air—so the athlete lands backward. Nobody had ever done it in competition. Button was in first place. Should he risk losing gold with the difficult jump? He took the challenge and did it—perfectly.

Dick Button, 1948

Button was the first American to capture figure-skating gold. Four years later, in Oslo, Norway, he'd repeat his victory with another groundbreaking move: the triple loop—a jump with three full spins.

"Now," Button said, "my mother never even mentions the piano."

Andrea Mead Lawrence, at nineteen, was a captain of the '52 US ski team. Alpine racing was second nature to Lawrence. She grew up in the mountains of Vermont, sometimes skiing down to the school bus.

Andrea Mead Lawrence

Back then, there were three separate alpine events (downhill, slalom, and giant slalom). In each type, skiers race down steep slopes against the clock, competing one at a time. No matter the event, every course has gates— actually flags set on poles to mark the route and show skiers where to turn. Lawrence took gold in the first event. Victory seemed guaranteed in her second race, too. But she fell—twice. She came in seventeenth place.

She had one more shot at gold. The event: the slalom.

In slalom, skiers weave around dozens of gates placed close together, making for tight turns around sharp corners. In Lawrence's first run, she missed a gate. She came to a complete stop. Then she backtracked to get on course. She didn't want to be disqualified.

Finally, she started—again. Somehow she finished fourth, only 1.2 seconds behind the leader. Could she make up the time in her second run?

All at once, the noise . . . the people . . . everything faded away. The only thing she saw was the quickest line down the course. Lawrence took off, smiling all the way to the finish line. She came in first and became the only US skier to win two gold medals in the same Olympics.

It's a record that has held—so far—for close to seventy years.

CHAPTER 4
1956–1968: Lights, Camera, Controversy

In 1956, the Games took place in northern Italy's Alps. For the first time, the Winter Olympics were broadcast live on TV across Western Europe.

More than eight hundred athletes came from thirty-two countries to compete—including, for the first time, the Soviet Union, a country made up of Russia and fourteen other states.

The Soviet Union team's entrance during the 1956 opening ceremony

At this time, no female figure skater from the United States had ever won gold. Maybe Tenley Albright, from Newton, Massachusetts, could.

Then, less than two weeks before her event, Albright stumbled during practice. A skate blade cut through her boot, leaving a deep gash in her ankle. But her father, who was a surgeon, "fixed me up," she said later. Albright's ankle was still too weak for spins or jumps. But she'd faced difficulty before. When she was eleven years old, she came down with polio, a disease that can paralyze a person. Luckily, Albright had a mild case. Ice skating made her muscles stronger.

On the morning of the event, Albright went through her moves. Her ankle held up. She was ready to compete. Albright didn't *just* compete. She took the lead going into the final performance. As she began skating to the music, something magical happened. Thousands of spectators began to sing along. They knew the song. This made Albright so happy, she forgot about her injury. She gave it her all and won.

Tenley Albright became the first American woman to take home gold in figure skating.

Tenley Albright, 1956 Games

Walt Disney

Four years later, the Games were on US soil again, in Squaw Valley, California. The famous film and TV producer Walt Disney, who was also a big skier, was in charge of the ceremonies. And for the first time, the Olympics were televised across the entire United States.

The 1964 Games in Innsbruck, Austria, came next. They went on despite the deaths of two athletes during practices. And during the 1968 Games, in Grenoble, France, one of the strangest

competitions in Olympic history took place.

Two skiers thought they'd won the slalom event. One was Jean-Claude Killy. At twenty-four,

Killy was already a hero in his home country, France. In 1968, he won two gold medals and was ready to win the last event to sweep the alpine triple. Only one skier could beat Killy: Austrian Karl Schranz.

Jean-Claude Killy

On the day of the race, thick fog covered the mountain. Killy had the fastest time after the first run. Schranz was just .32 seconds behind. In the second run, Killy went first. Then the fog grew worse. Some of the skiers following Killy fell or missed gates.

Finally it was Schranz's turn. He started on his run. Later he said that midway down the run, "I saw this shadow walking across the course. There was no way I could continue." The Austrian team claimed it was a police officer. Two officials and another skier agreed. Schranz redid his turn. His combined time: 24 hundredths of a second faster than Killy's.

The French team protested. Schranz had missed two gates in his first try before he stopped. They wondered if he had made up the whole story. They thought the gold belonged to Killy. A jury met for hours. Finally, the decision was announced. Killy earned the medal.

He won triple gold and retired. Schranz could only hope his time would come at the next Olympics.

To this day, nobody knows what really happened.

Karl Schranz (middle)

CHAPTER 5
The '70s: Jumps and Spins for the Win

It was 1972. For the first time, the Winter Games took place in Asia. The city of Sapporo, in Japan, hosted the competition. Karl Schranz

was now thirty-three years old. This was his last chance for gold. Then, three days before the Olympics, he was banned from the Games.

Why?

At the time, only amateur athletes were allowed to compete. The Olympic committee said companies were paying Schranz to use their equipment. That made him a pro.

Opening ceremony at the 1972 Games

Earlier, Schranz had spoken out against the policy. Like many Olympians, he'd grown up poor. Schranz needed the money to keep skiing. Back in Austria, a hundred thousand fans greeted him at the airport. There was a parade in his honor. Even without a medal, Schranz was a hero.

Japan, meanwhile, desperately wanted a gold medal, something that had yet to happen at the Winter Games. As hosts, gold would mean so much. Their best chance rested on ski jumper Yukio Kasaya. In the event, athletes ski off a curved ramp, soaring into the air before landing. They try for the longest leap with the best form, with scores based on distance *and* style.

Now Kasaya got into starting position. He sped down the ramp, going faster and faster. Then he lifted off. Leaning forward, his skis side by side in two straight lines, he stayed in perfect form.

Yukio Kasaya

Kasaya jumped 84 meters (275.6 feet). It was the longest leap in the round. He received the highest style score as well, 57 out of 60 points. Then he won the second round, too.

Ski jumping turned out to be a Japanese sweep: gold for Kasaya, silver and bronze for his teammates. The fans went wild. In time, Kasaya was honored with his own stamp. But all three skiers won Japanese hearts.

Winners in 70m ski jump, 1972 Winter Olympic Games

In 1976, the Games were again held in Innsbruck, Austria. Dorothy Hamill, the top figure skater from the United States, appeared in her first Olympics. Already Hamill was known for two things: her signature haircut (cut short to stay out of her eyes) and inventing her own powerful moves. Her most famous was the "Hamill camel." It started with the classic camel spin, with the skater extending one leg backward, so the body looks like a "T." But Hamill added a sit spin at the end.

Going into the final program, she was in first place.

Hamill skated onto the ice, looking calm but feeling nervous. As the music began, however, she skated perfectly—Hamill camel and all. Every judge gave her first place. Hamill was a sensation. Millions of American girls and women cut their hair just like hers. That same year,

Hamill turned pro, the first female athlete in any sport to sign a million-dollar contract with a company. She performed with the Ice Capades, a theatrical ice show, then went on to buy the business.

CHAPTER 6
1980–1984: Miracles and More

Lake Placid hosted again in 1980, this time with archenemies—the United States and Soviet Union—facing off in hockey. It was the semifinal round. The winning team would play for gold.

It was a matter of national pride for each country. The Soviet team was thought to be the best in the world. The US team was made up of a lot of college students. They were ranked seventh out of the twelve teams. Yet, somehow, they'd made it this far.

After two periods passed, the score was 3–2. The Americans were down by one goal. That was

all. Eight minutes and thirty-nine seconds into the third period, the United States scored. Now the game was tied.

The puck slid toward US captain Mike Eruzione. Quickly, he trapped it. A Soviet defenseman skated between Eruzione and the net. Should he pass? Then he realized the goalie couldn't see the puck. Eruzione fired his shot.

Men's hockey: United States vs. Soviet Union, 1980

He scored!

The United States had the lead, 4–3. The Soviets kept shooting. Each time, goalie Jim Craig stopped the puck. Now there were five seconds left. Announcer Al Michaels shouted, "Do you believe in miracles?" With one second on the clock, he answered, "Yes!"

The US team won! The crowd went wild.

The team went on to the final match against Finland and ended up with a gold medal.

American speed skater Eric Heiden was at the US-Soviet game, cheering every play. Heiden had already won four events, breaking records every time. He had one last race the next morning: the final in the 10,000-meter (6.2 miles). Heiden couldn't sleep; he was that excited about the hockey match. Then he overslept. Grabbing some bread, he hurried to the track.

How would he compete?

Eric Heiden

Amazingly, his time set a world record: 14 minutes, 28.13 seconds. And in the end, he took first place. Eric Heiden became the first person in Olympic history—Summer or Winter—to win five individual gold medals.

The fourteenth Winter Olympics were held in 1984. All was peaceful in Sarajevo, the host city in a European country called Yugoslavia.

Sarajevo and the Bosnian War, 1992–1995

Eight years after the '84 Olympics, different regions of Yugoslavia declared independence from the Communist government. Fighting and bloodshed followed; Muslim populations were targeted. Sarajevo, now in the new country of Bosnia and Herzegovina, was hit hard. On the tenth anniversary of the Sarajevo Games, fighting still raged. The '94 Olympics dedicated its opening and closing ceremonies to the war-torn city. Almost two years later, peace was finally declared.

Present-day Bosnia and Herzegovina

One of the biggest draws at these Games was ice dancing.

The event is a skating contest for partners. There are no trick jumps or high lifts. It's all about dancing—grace, rhythm, and style. Sound simple? It's not. There are strict rules. The pair always needs to move forward. Most of the time they have to skate face-to-face, so close their skates practically touch. On the day of their event, British partners Jayne Torvill and Christopher Dean went to the ice arena at six in the morning to practice. The pair skated to a piece of classical music called *Boléro*.

When they finished, they looked up to see the entire cleaning staff giving them a standing ovation.

Would the judges feel the same way?

Yes! Torvill and Dean earned gold—and the first perfect scores for presentation in the history of Olympic figure skating.

CHAPTER 7
1988: Battles, Bumps, and Bruises

After winning silver in 1984, Canadian figure skater Brian Orser was hoping for gold in 1988 at Calgary, the first Winter Games in his home country. The Olympics went down in history as the "Battle of the Brians." American Brian Boitano was the other favorite and a good friend of Orser's. The free skate program—

Brian Boitano   Brian Orser

four and half minutes long—would decide the gold medal winner. Before the event, the Brians came face-to-face backstage. They exchanged punches. Reporters rushed over. Of course it was a joke.

The final program had required "elements"—moves skaters must do, certain spins and jumps.

One was the triple axel, the trickiest jump of all at the time. Get it right, and your score went up. Boitano nailed two. His routine was just about perfect. Boitano felt too nervous to watch Orser perform. He only heard Orser's score from the final judge. A perfect six. Boitano braced himself for silver. Because of his difficult moves, however, the judges awarded him higher marks. For the American, nabbing gold was great, but also a bittersweet victory. His buddy Brian had lost.

In the women's event, the top two skaters didn't share a name. They shared the same music. Their choice for the last program was from the opera *Carmen*. East Germany's Katarina Witt was graceful and artistic. (East Germany and West Germany did not reunite into one country until October 1990.) Still, her scores left room for American skater Debi Thomas to take gold. Few African Americans competed in winter sports. Thomas was a young skater of color, excelling in competitions where everyone else was white.

Her goal was to be an Olympian. Now, almost twenty-one and studying to be a doctor, Thomas was competing at the Calgary Games.

About three minutes into her performance, Thomas landed badly after a jump. "The whole reason for being here was to skate great," she said

Katarina Witt   Debi Thomas

later. "And if it was like, I couldn't skate great, I didn't want to be out there."

In the end, Witt took gold, Thomas bronze. Debi Thomas still made history. She became the first Black athlete to win a medal in the Winter Games. She broke the color barrier and paved the way for Kristi Yamaguchi, the first Asian American to win gold at the Winter Olympics, in 1992.

Another historic first in Calgary was the Jamaica bobsled team.

Many laughed. How would athletes from a tropical island compete in this winter sport? Some of the men had never seen a sled before signing up for the team. But five months later, they were at the Olympics.

The first event was the two-man bobsled. Amazingly, the Jamaican pair beat ten other teams. Now they wanted to compete in the four-man race. They had enough men, but they didn't have the bigger sled needed. Quickly, the team created Jamaican Bobsled T-shirts, sweatshirts, and souvenirs. Word spread. The items sold fast. The team bought a sled. Forty thousand people lined the track to cheer them on. In the third run, the bobsledders got off to a quick start, reaching a top speed of eighty-five miles per hour.

Suddenly, disaster struck.

They hit a wall, and a moment later they hit it again. The sled tipped over. The athletes crawled out—they were okay. But their race was over. As they walked with the sled down the track, fans reached out to shake their hands. "We love you!" they shouted. The team finished the race—their way.

The 1988 Jamaican bobsled team came in last place. But their story inspired a Disney movie about a bobsled team who followed their dream.

CHAPTER 8
1992–1994: Comebacks and Crime

Bonnie Blair was already a star when she arrived in Albertville, France, for the 1992 Winter Games. The American speed skater had won two medals—gold and bronze—in Calgary. On Christmas Day 1989, her father died, and Blair had stopped training for a while. Blair's dad had always been sure she'd be an Olympic champion. He'd led the Blair Bunch, a large group of family and friends who traveled to her competitions. Charles Blair wouldn't be in Albertville now. But the Blair Bunch was, with her mom leading the gang. Bonnie Blair's love for the sport helped her overcome her grief, and she left the Games with two more gold medals.

She would go on to win the 500-meter and

Bonnie Blair taking the lead in a race at the 1992 Winter Olympics

1,000-meter races at the next Olympics, making Blair the first US woman to capture five gold medals and the first American Winter athlete to earn six career medals. Her record-breaking performance came in 1994. That was only two years after the Albertville Games.

Why?

Organizers had decided to hold Summer and Winter Games in different years. They felt it would bring more attention to the smaller cold-weather competition. This time the Winter Games were

in Lillehammer, Norway. A few years before, the Soviet Union had broken apart. Russia, the largest and most powerful of the now-independent states, was competing on its own for the first time.

1994 Winter Olympics in Lillehammer, Norway

The Russian team won an outstanding eleven events, including every figure-skating competition but one. Women's singles.

The top American skaters were Nancy Kerrigan and Tonya Harding. Reporters followed them everywhere. It had little to do with skating. The women came from different backgrounds.

Nancy Kerrigan (middle) with her parents

Kerrigan had a close-knit family. They supported her every step of the way. She'd already won a bronze medal in 1992. Harding had a tough childhood and hadn't finished high school. At the previous Olympics, in Albertville, she'd come in right behind Kerrigan.

Tonya Harding at the 1992 Games

Before the Lillehammer Olympics, something shocking had happened at the US Figure Skating Championships in Detroit, Michigan. The winner and runner-up would go to Norway. After one practice, a man attacked Kerrigan, striking her above the right knee. Kerrigan couldn't compete.

Harding easily won the championship. She was going to the Olympics.

But what about Kerrigan? Officials decided that she was a special case. They gave her the second spot. Then things got really weird. Police discovered that Harding's ex-husband had hired the attacker. Harding claimed she only found that out after Kerrigan was hurt. So in the end, both skaters went to Lillehammer.

So did sixteen-year-old Oksana Baiul from Ukraine.

Baiul, too, had struggled growing up. Her coach was all the family she had. Nevertheless, Baiul was a natural performer and had just won the World Championship. At Lillehammer, the first program turned out to be the most watched sports event ever. Kerrigan placed first, Baiul second. But the free skate was still to come. (As for Harding, she hadn't performed as well as they had and was out of the medal race.)

In her final routine, Kerrigan's skating was almost perfect. Baiul also gave a lovely, graceful performance.

Oksana Baiul

It would be close.

Four judges voted for Kerrigan, five for Baiul. The difference was one-tenth of a point. Baiul won gold, Kerrigan took silver.

Later, new evidence against Harding came to light. It showed she'd been in on the attack all along. The US Figure Skating Association banned her for life. Tonya Harding could never compete again. It was a shameful story, going against everything the Olympics stood for.

CHAPTER 9
1998: Olympic Firsts

The Olympic decade closed with the '98 Games in Nagano, Japan. For the first time, pro athletes could compete, and snowboard events were now part of the program.

Another first at the Olympics: women's hockey. In Nagano, the United States and Canada made it to the final match. The competition between them was fierce. "You could say there is an intense dislike," according to Canadian coach Shannon Miller.

With four minutes left in the game, the United States led 2–1. The Canadian coach pulled the goalie to put an extra scorer on the ice. The strategy didn't work. The US team scored again. The game ended 3–1. The American team celebrated wildly. The Canadian team, winning silver, stood quietly off to the side. Their disappointment was deep.

Yet it was a triumph for both the United States and Canada. There had been no hockey teams for girls when these players were growing up. Now not only were they Olympians, both teams were medal winners.

Meanwhile, two American figure skaters were once again vying for gold: seventeen-year-old Michelle Kwan and Tara Lipinski, only fifteen.

Michelle Kwan   Tara Lipinski

Kwan went first in the four-minute-thirty-second-long free skate program, nailing seven jumps with three full spins in the air. It was a gold-medal performance. But then it was Lipinski's turn. Right from the start, she skated joyfully and full of life. She took off for a backward jump, spinning three times in the air, landing perfectly.

Snowboarding

Snowboarding dates back to the 1960s, when an American inventor fastened skis together so they'd work like a surfboard or skateboard, only on snow. The sport took off, and by the 1980s, there were world competitions. Some skiers believed that snowboarders—mostly young people—weren't serious athletes. But snowboarding became so popular, the International Olympic Committee moved to include the sport in the Games.

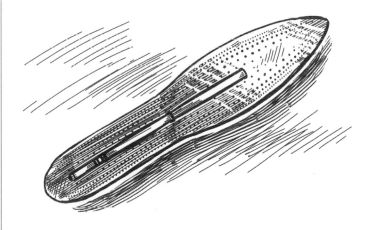

Immediately, she did it again. The element was her special move. At the end—the toughest moment of any routine—Lipinski went for another tricky combination. A triple jump followed by a full spin, followed by another triple . . . lifting off from just the edge of her skate, Lipinski propelled herself high into the air.

"She pulls it off!" the announcer shouted.

Tara Lipinski became the youngest athlete to ever win gold in an individual event, beating Sonja Henie by two months.

CHAPTER 10
2002: Sleds, Skates, and New Sports

The world had changed after the deadly attacks on the United States in September 2001. One flag was found amid the wreckage of New York City's fallen Twin Towers. Although torn and tattered, it was still in one piece. Five months later, at the 2002 Winter Games in Salt Lake City, Utah,

Twin Towers, New York City

the US Olympic team, along with New York City police and firefighters, carried that flag in the opening ceremony. It stood for everything the country had been through and how it was trying to heal.

The Olympics continued, bigger than ever. There were seventy-eight events now. And for the first time, women were competing in bobsled.

Speed skating at the Winter Olympics, 1924

US bobsled team led by Billy Fiske, 1932

French skier Jean-Claude Killy, 1968

Japanese skier Yukio Kasaya in the 90-meter ski jump, 1972

US figure skater Dorothy Hamill, 1976

Tom Sweeney/Star Tribune/Getty Images

US hockey team at the 1980 Winter Olympics

Steve Powell/Getty Images Sport/Getty Images North America/Getty Images

US hockey team after the "Miracle on Ice" win, 1980

US skater Eric Heiden (back) in the men's
500-meter speed-skating event, 1980

Jayne Torvill and Christopher Dean in the ice-dancing event, 1984

US figure skater Kristi Yamaguchi, 1992

The Jamaican bobsled team starting their race, 1988

The Jamaican bobsled team crashes, 1988.

US figure skaters Tonya Harding (front) and Nancy Kerrigan, 1994 Winter Olympics

Nancy Kerrigan wins a silver medal, 1994.

Freestyle skiing competition, 1998

Snowboarding event, 1998

Opening ceremony in Salt Lake City, Utah, 2002

Apolo Ohno (front), 2002 Winter Olympics

Lindsey Jacobellis (middle), 2006 Winter Olympics

US skier Bode Miller, 2014

Women's cross-country team sprint freestyle race, 2018 Winter Olympics

American Vonetta Flowers had always dreamed of going to the Olympics. She'd been a track star in school. When she didn't qualify for the Summer Games, she turned to a new sport, one that needed strength and speed, too.

She became a brakewoman in bobsled. Flowers paired with pilot Jill Bakken. No one expected them to win. A German team on their first run had already broken the track "push record" with a time of 5.32 seconds. (The "push" is the takeoff of the race.)

Now it was Flowers and Bakken's turn to push the sled along the flat top of the course. The faster the athletes ran before the starting line, the faster the sled would go. Bakken hopped in from the side. Flowers kept going, giving one final push. Then she jumped in from the back. They bettered the German record with 5.31 seconds. The pair continued, flying down the track at eighty miles per hour, whipping around each curve and turn.

Bakken steered with skill and daring. At the end, Flowers pulled the brake lever. The sled slowed to a stop. They had the best run time, too.

In their second try, the Germans again performed with amazing strength. The pressure was back on Flowers and Bakken now. Could they power through with a faster time than their rivals?

Yes! They edged out the Germans by three-tenths of a second. The bobsled victory broke a forty-six-year drought for the United States. And Flowers became the first Black athlete to win gold at the Winter Games. At the finish line, she wept with joy.

Vonetta Flowers

The next day, the skeleton race was held on the same course. This sledding event had only taken place twice before, once in 1928 and again in 1948. In skeleton, a slider starts out in a crouch, holding on to the sides of the flat, heavy sled. Then the athlete sprints, sliding the sled on the ice, then leaping onto the sled face-first. They race with their chins almost touching the ice, their arms pressed tightly to their sides.

Skeleton race

Jim Shea Jr. was representing the United States. Back in 1964, his dad competed in cross-country skiing. *Way* back in 1932, his grandfather Jack—who'd boycotted the Olympics in Nazi Germany—won his two gold medals. Jack Shea planned to be at his grandson's race. Sadly, he died seventeen days before the opening ceremonies. In a way, he was still with the younger Shea, who kept his grandfather's photo inside his helmet. And he won gold by five-hundredths of a second.

At a different arena—the ice rink—Canadians Jamie Salé and David Pelletier had the audience on its feet, too. It was the final program of the pairs figure-skating competition. Unlike ice dancing, pairs is all about thrilling jumps and spins, with the male skater holding his partner high above his head in lifts, and even tossing her in the air. Salé and Pelletier's routine was set to music from the movie *Love Story*.

Jamie Salé and David Pelletier

"Six! Six! Six!" the crowd cried, demanding a perfect score. But the gold went to Russian skaters instead. "How did that happen?" an announcer stammered.

One judge had been pressured to vote for the Russians. The upshot was that the Canadians ended up receiving gold medals, too. The Russians kept theirs as well. Was that fair? You decide.

Meanwhile, short track speed skating—an official Olympic sport since 1992—was proving to be a crowd-pleaser.

Apolo Ohno

In short track races, anything can happen. Racers bump and crash off course. That's why nineteen-year-old American Apolo Ohno loved the sport. He was the favorite in the 1,000-meter event.

Short Track, Long Track—
What's the Difference?

In long track races, the oval is almost four times longer than a short track oval. Long track racers, each in a separate lane, are all about speed on long straightaways. On the short track, turns make up most of the race. Athletes skate in packs, figuring out when to pass, placing their hands on the ice to balance on every tight corner.

Short track race

Steven Bradbury

Steven Bradbury of Australia was also in the race. It was his fourth Olympics. He'd never placed higher than eighth in an individual event. But his plan was to avoid trouble by staying behind the pack.

Bradbury and Ohno both made the final. At the starting gun, five men took off. "Four-man pack with Bradbury hanging behind," the announcer said. At the final curve, Ohno was in first place. One skater tried to pass him. They both spun out. Two more fell in a chain reaction.

Suddenly, Bradbury had a clear path. He crossed the finish line, surprised. Had he really won? he wondered. Yes! Australia had its first ever Winter gold.

As for Ohno, he scrambled and slid across the ice on his hands and knees for second place.

The next event was the 1,500-meter. For most of the race, Ohno stayed in last place. His strategy, like Bradbury's, was to play it safe. With two laps to go, he picked up speed, passing skaters. Now the final curve was ahead. Only one man was in front of Ohno. Ohno tried to pass. Korean skater Kim Dong-sung blocked the move.

He crossed the line first. Sure of his victory, he began his victory lap.

But Kim was disqualified for the block.

Ohno won gold. He'd go on to win six more medals in 2006 and 2010. When he retired, he was the most decorated American Winter Olympian.

CHAPTER 11
2006–2010: Legends and Losses

Years earlier, Apolo Ohno had trained with a good friend, Shani Davis. Davis came to his first Olympics in 2006, skating long track.

That year, the Games were in Turin, Italy.

In his very first Olympic event, the 1,000-meter race, Davis made history. He became the first Black man to win an individual medal at the Winter Olympics—and the medal was gold! Davis earned silver in the 1,500-meter, too. Four years later he repeated the exact same wins.

Shani Davis

Davis competed one last time in 2018. His legacy includes not only four medals but a Shani Davis statue at the Smithsonian National Museum of African American History and Culture in Washington, DC.

It was at Turin that snowboard cross became an official sport. In the speed event, four riders race at a time, whizzing down an obstacle-like course with turns and jumps. American Lindsey Jacobellis seemed destined for gold. In the final,

Jacobellis took an early lead and held it. At the next-to-the-last jump, she decided to have a little fun with a cool move. So she reached for a board grab on the jump. All at once, Jacobellis fell sideways. She righted herself. But it was too late. Another snowboarder zipped past to capture gold. Jacobellis took silver.

Jacobellis was only twenty years old with an Olympics future ahead of her. She competed in three more Games, but never made it to the Olympic podium again. It never stopped her. She won every other snowboard cross contest—

again and again. One reporter noted after her final race, "Jacobellis is the best her sport has seen."

Lindsey Vonn

In 2010, American skier Lindsey Vonn also had yet to medal after competing in two Olympics. At twenty-five, in Vancouver, Canada, Vonn was back again. This time she was a favorite for gold in downhill. Then a week before the Games, she bruised her shin. It was hard to even put on a ski boot.

Vancouver's course was one of the toughest in the world. And the race is an all-out test of speed—one run, one chance. Skiers need to be in top shape. But Vonn got lucky. Bad weather caused delays. By race day, the sky was clear, and Vonn had recovered enough to compete.

Her biggest rival was teammate Julia Mancuso. Mancuso had already earned gold in 2006's giant slalom event. Now she skied first. Her time was great: 1 minute, 44.75 seconds.

Vonn had the quicker start, though, and attacked every inch of the course. As she neared the finish line, cowbells rang. People shouted. She whizzed past a sign that read "Vonn-couver."

Her time: 1 minute, 44.19 seconds. Vonn was the first American woman to win gold in downhill. With expectations high for Vonn to win five races, she left with just one more, a bronze. But the skier had done exactly what she'd set out to do. She gave it all she had.

CHAPTER 12
2014: Emotions Run High

In 2014, Sochi hosted the first Winter Olympics held in Russia. Just across its border, Ukraine was in crisis. Ukrainians were protesting government policies. The unrest turned deadly. On February 20, the capital burned. Dozens of protesters were killed.

The next day, in Sochi, four Ukrainian athletes were competing in the biathlon relay. The biathlon is a skiing and rifle-shooting contest. In the relay, teammates take turns skiing laps, stopping at different points to shoot at targets. The Ukrainian team wasn't very fast. But they were steady. Sometimes that's enough. Captain Olena Pidhrushna took the final lap. She crossed the finish line in first place. Then she sprawled in the snow, tired from the race and so much more. The athletes asked for a moment of silence to honor the dead. With tears in their eyes, they dedicated the victory to "the whole of Ukraine."

On the slopes, another skier—American Bode Miller—readied himself for his final Olympic race. Bode had already seen alpine triumph, with five medals. Yet he'd won nothing at all at the 2006 Games. He was back simply because he loved to ski fast. Miller had been through a lot that year. His younger brother, Chelone "Chilly" Miller, had died. This Olympics was really important to Bode Miller, as it was his fifth and last.

Bode Miller with his younger brother, Chilly

Miller didn't medal in his first events. Then it was time for the super-G, the super giant slalom. The race falls somewhere between downhill and giant slalom—a mix of speed and technical skill with thirty-five or so gates and just one run. Miller hurtled down the mountain, almost out of control. Somehow he held it together.

He made it to the finish line in 1 minute, 18.67 seconds. Miller tied for bronze, and emotion washed over him. The end of his Olympic career . . . the loss of Chilly. Miller couldn't help but cry. Later he tweeted, "Thanks for all the support. . . . I miss my brother."

In that one race Miller broke two records: He was the oldest alpine skier to win a medal and had won the most medals of any US skier.

CHAPTER 13
2018: Two Sports, One Athlete— Two Athletes, One Sport

The 2018 Olympics in PyeongChang, South Korea, were all about excitement.

First, a scandal: Russia was banned from the Games. Its government was found guilty of giving athletes drugs to make them stronger. Then, a reunion: Decades ago, rival countries North and South Korea had been one nation. After the split, the two have been in conflict. But in PyeongChang, women from both countries joined together to play hockey. There was one unified Korean team. The team came in last, but it gave hope to both sides for the future.

What else did the twenty-third competition deliver? A first-time Olympian who did what no other athlete had done before. Ester Ledecka, from the Czech Republic, competed in ski *and* snowboard events. Growing up, everyone told her to focus on one sport. It would be too difficult to excel in two. But Ledecka stood firm, doing what she loved. Both sports. How would she manage in the Olympics?

North and South Korea joined to form a unified women's hockey team in 2018.

For Ledecka, the skiing event—the super-G—
was more challenging. She'd never placed higher
than nineteenth in any international competition.
Ledecka crossed the line in 1 minute, 21.11
seconds. *That can't be right,* she thought.
It was way too fast, a gold medal time. She stared
at the scoreboard, waiting for the numbers to
change. They didn't. She'd really come in first.

Next up, snowboarding's giant parallel slalom.
In this contest, two riders at a time race down side-
by-side courses. The fastest time of all the heats
wins. Looking for gold again, Ledecka started
quicker than her opponent. She stayed ahead,
but not by much. Selina Joerg from Germany was
catching up. Near the end, Ledecka turned on the
speed. She widened the gap.

"Super-G gold! Snowboarding gold!!" the
announcer shouted. "Things like that are just
not supposed to happen. Ester Ledecka has taken
double gold!"

Like Ledecka, the US women's cross-country ski team had no idea what would happen in South Korea. They'd never won a single medal.

Thirty-five-year-old Kikkan Randall was about to start her eighteenth Olympic event, the team sprint. Her partner: twenty-six-year-old Jessie Diggins. Growing up, Diggins had a Kikkan Randall poster hanging on her wall. Now they were competing together. The hilly course was about three-quarters of a mile. Both skiers would race three laps, switching off after each one. In the final, ten teams took off at the starting gun. On Randall's last lap, she pushed ahead into third place. Now it was up to Diggins.

Diggins knew they'd at least get bronze. She decided to go for gold.

Going into the stadium, she passed Norway's Marit Bjørgen. Bjørgen was a legend. If Diggins could beat her, she could beat just about anybody. But Sweden was still in first, going into the final straight. Diggins pushed harder. She drew even with the leader. Right at the finish, she threw one leg over the line. Then she fell to the ground. Randall rushed over. "Did we just win the Olympics?" Diggins gasped.

"Yeah!" screamed Randall. The relay was her last race—ever. "It's the best ending I could have asked for," she said.

Of course the Olympics never really end . . .

Jessie Diggins and Kikkan Randall

CHAPTER 14
The Spirit Continues

The Games go on, decade after decade, with a spirit that reaches beyond sports. Men and women help opponents. Athletes congratulate rivals. Coaches share equipment.

And they take that spirit with them, outside the Games.

Legendary Norwegian speed skater Johann Koss broke every record in long track, winning five medals along the way. He gave his '94 gold-medal prize money to Olympic Aid, to help bring sports to children in need. Later, he turned the organization into an even bigger force for good. His Right to Play charity helps 2.3 million children every year.

Johann Koss in Tanzania with Right to Play participants, 2010

Alpine skier Andrea Mead Lawrence went on to help pass California's environmental laws, still in effect today. Winter Olympians have worked hard to raise awareness on gay rights and equality for women. They've started foundations and written books.

At the Games in Beijing, China, in 2022, there will be a record 109 events and a record number of women athletes. Who will soar? Who will score? Who will do the impossible on the slopes and on the ice?

You never know what Olympians can achieve.

BEIJING 2022

Timeline of the Winter Olympics

1924 — First Winter Olympics take place in Chamonix, France

1936 — Despite boycott threats, Olympics are held in Nazi Germany

1948 — Olympics continue after twelve-year break due to World War II

1980 — The US hockey team performs a miracle, defeating the top-ranked Soviet Union

1988 — Debi Thomas wins bronze in women's figure skating, becoming the first Black athlete to medal at the Winter Games

1992 — Kristi Yamaguchi becomes the first Asian American to win Winter gold

1994 — Nancy Kerrigan hurt in an attack arranged by Tonya Harding's ex-husband

1998 — Snowboarding debuts

2010 — Short track speed skater Apolo Ohno becomes the most decorated American Winter Olympian; skier Lindsey Vonn is the first American woman to win the downhill event

2018 — North Korea and South Korea field a unified team in women's hockey

Timeline of the World

1924 — President Calvin Coolidge signs the Indian Citizenship Act, declaring all Native Americans to be American citizens

1948 — The country of Israel is created on May 14

1952 — *The Diary of Anne Frank* is published for the first time in the United States

1960 — Black college students stage first civil rights protest at a segregated Woolworth's counter in Greensboro, North Carolina

1968 — First 911 emergency phone system is established in Haleyville, Alabama, on February 16

1972 — Legendary video game company Atari—developers of *Pac-Man* and *Space Invaders*—is founded

1980 — Mount St. Helens erupts in Washington State on May 18, killing fifty-seven people and spreading ash around twenty-two-thousand square miles

1994 — On May 10, Nelson Mandela is inaugurated, making him the first Black president of South Africa

1998 — Google is founded by Larry Page and Sergey Brin

2010 — The Apple iPad goes on sale in April

2018 — Stan Lee—co-creator of Spider-Man, the Hulk, and the Fantastic Four—dies at ninety-five

Bibliography

*Books for young readers

Bull, Andy. *Speed Kings: The 1932 Winter Olympics and the Fastest Men in the World.* New York: Avery Books, 2015.

Diggins, Jessie, and Todd Smith. *Brave Enough.* Minneapolis: University of Minnesota Press, 2020.

Eruzione, Mike, and Neal Boudette. *The Making of a Miracle: The Untold Story of the Captain of the 1980 Gold Medal–Winning US Olympic Hockey Team*. New York: HarperCollins, 2020.

Greenspan, Bud. *Frozen in Time: The Greatest Moments at the Winter Olympics*. Santa Monica, CA: General Publishing Group, 1997.

*Lipinski, Tara, and Emily Costello. *Triumph on Ice: An Autobiography*. New York: Bantam, 1997.

Wallechinsky, David, and Jaime Loucky. *The Complete Book of the Winter Olympics, 2014 Edition*. Hertford, NC: Crossroad Press, 2014.

Websites

www.olympic.org (International Olympic Committee)

www.teamusa.org (United States Olympic & Paralympic Committee)